WE WISH YOU
A MERRY CHRISTMAS

SONGS OF THE SEASON
FOR YOUNG PEOPLE

ARRANGED BY
DAN FOX

THE METROPOLITAN MUSEUM OF ART
NEW YORK

ARCADE PUBLISHING
NEW YORK

LITTLE, BROWN AND COMPANY

Copyright © 1989 by The Metropolitan Museum of Art
All rights reserved, including the right to reproduce this book or portions thereof in any form.
Published by The Metropolitan Museum of Art, New York, and Arcade Publishing, Inc., New York, a Little, Brown company.
Published simultaneously in Canada by Little, Brown & Company (Canada) Limited.

Produced by the Department of Special Publications,
The Metropolitan Museum of Art
Photography by The Metropolitan Museum of Art Photograph Studio
Music engraved by W. R. Music Service, New York
Printed and bound in Japan by Dai Nippon Printing Co., Ltd.
Designed by Miriam Berman

Library of Congress Catalog Card Number 89-84225
Library of Congress Cataloging-in-Publication Data is available.

BOMC offers recordings and compact discs, cassettes
and records. For information and catalog write to
BOMR, Camp Hill, PA 17012.

ISBN 0-87099-552-9 (MMA)
ISBN 1-55970-043-2 (Arcade)

1 3 5 7 9 10 8 6 4 2

CONTENTS

The Christmas Tree.
J. Alden Weir,
American,
1852–1919.
Oil on canvas, 1890.

PREFACE

WE WISH YOU A MERRY CHRISTMAS presents twenty-five classic holiday songs from England, Wales, France, Germany, and America. The music dates from the Middle Ages to the twentieth century and the songs express the many moods of the Christmas season: from solemn to festive, from gentle to triumphant, from quiet to exuberant. The musical arrangements are simple and easy to follow, suitable for beginning to intermediate musicians.

All of the songs in the book have been imaginatively coupled with one or more works from the collections of The Metropolitan Museum of Art in New York—paintings, drawings, lithographs, woodcuts, tapestries, sculpture, stained glass, tiles, and illuminated manuscripts. The art spans more than five hundred years and comes from many countries—Germany, France, Italy, Austria, England, Switzerland, Egypt, Belgium, Holland, and America. It ranges from paintings of the Nativity by unknown Renaissance artists to masterpieces of the same subject by Hieronymus Bosch and François Boucher; from sixth-century Egyptian textiles to elaborate silk embroideries made in England eleven centuries later; and from simple medieval woodcuts to colorful lithographs of the twentieth century.

It is our hope that the diversity of the art, the selection of the songs, and the simplicity of the arrangements will enhance the enjoyment of the holiday season.

A NOTE ON THE MUSIC

Each of the songs includes guitar chords that can be used for easy accompaniment; a fingering chart appears on page 80. When an arrangement is in a key that is awkward for the guitar, capo instructions and alternate chords are provided. After the capo is in place, the song should be played using the chords that appear in parentheses.

The music is suitable not only for piano and guitar, but also for other C instruments, such as the violin, flute, and recorder. Players of these instruments should read the highest notes in the upper staff.

Away in a Manger

Andante

Traditional

1. A - way in a man - ger no crib for a
2. The cat - tle are low - ing, the Ba - by a -
3. Be near me, Lord Je - sus, I ask Thee to

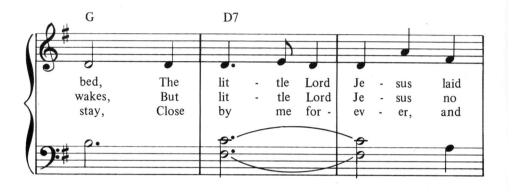

bed, The lit - tle Lord Je - sus laid
wakes, But lit - tle Lord Je - sus no
stay, Close by me for - ev - er, and

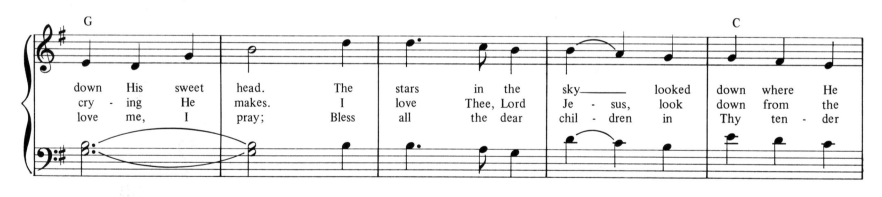

down His sweet head. The stars in the sky looked down where He
cry - ing He makes. I love Thee, Lord Je - sus, look down from the
love me, I pray; Bless all the dear chil - dren in Thy ten - der

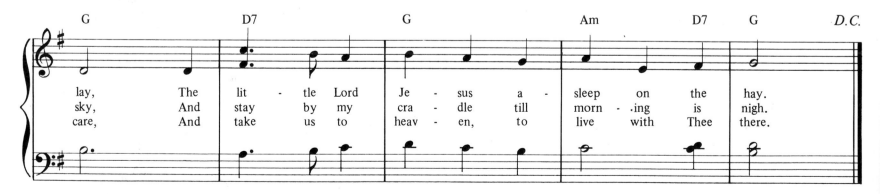

lay, The lit - tle Lord Je - sus a - sleep on the hay.
sky, And stay by my cra - dle till morn - ing is nigh.
care, And take us to heav - en, to live with Thee there.

D.C.

Details of two stained-glass windows from the Carmelite Church at Boppard-on-the-Rhine. German, 1440–46.

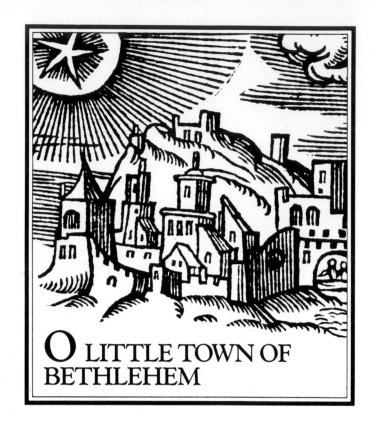

O LITTLE TOWN OF BETHLEHEM

Words by Phillips Brooks
Music by Lewis H. Redner

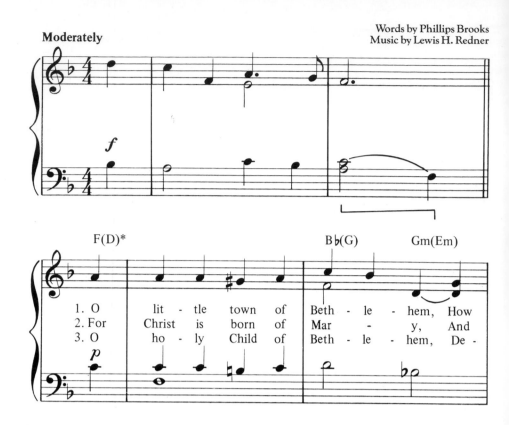

1. O lit - tle town of Beth - le - hem, How
2. For Christ is born of Mar - y, And
3. O ho - ly Child of Beth - le - hem, De -

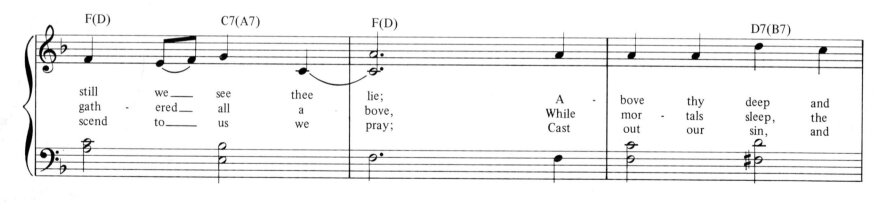

still we see thee lie; A - bove thy deep and
gath - ered all a - bove, While mor - tals our sleep, the
scend to us we pray; Cast out our sin, and

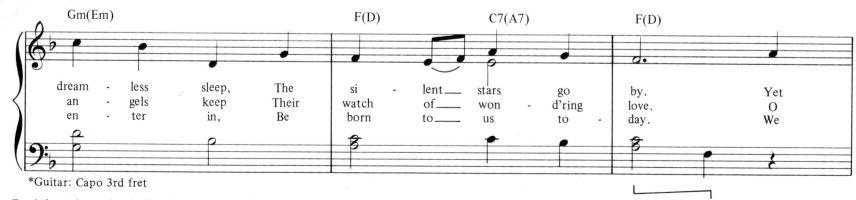

dream - less sleep, The si - lent stars go by. Yet
an - gels keep in, Their watch of won - d'ring love. O
en - ter in, Be born to us to - day. We

*Guitar: Capo 3rd fret

Detail of a woodcut attributed to Jean Cousin the Younger, French, 1522–1594.
From *Figures de la Saincte Bible accompagnées de briefs discours . . .*, published by Jean Le Clerc, Paris, 1614.

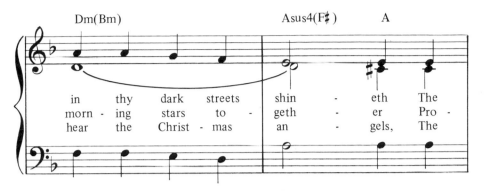

Dm(Bm)   Asus4(F♯)   A

in   thy   dark   streets   shin - eth   The
morn - ing   stars   to - geth - er   Pro -
hear   the   Christ - mas   an - gels,   The

Dm(Bm)   (A)   (Dm)   (Gm)   A(F♯)

ev - er - last - ing   Light;   The
claim   the   ho - ly   birth,   And
great   glad   ti - dings   tell;   O

cresc.   *f*   *p*

F(D)   B♭(G)

hopes   and   fears   of   all   the   years   Are
prais - es   sing   to   God   the   King,   And
come   to   us,   a - bide   with   us,   Our

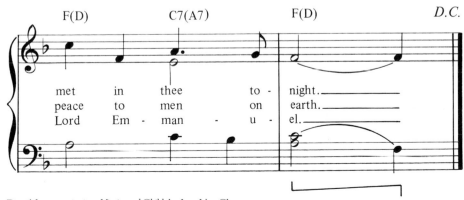

F(D)   C7(A7)   F(D)   *D.C.*

met   in   thee   to - night._____
peace   to   men   on   earth._____
Lord   Em - man - u - el._____

Detail from a painting, *Virgin and Child,* by Joos Van Cleve,
Flemish, active by 1507, d. 1540/41. Tempera and oil on wood.

SILENT NIGHT

Words adapted from the German of Joseph Mohr
Music by Franz Grüber

Quietly

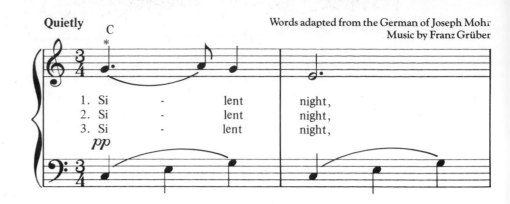

1. Si - lent night,
2. Si - lent night,
3. Si - lent night,

pp

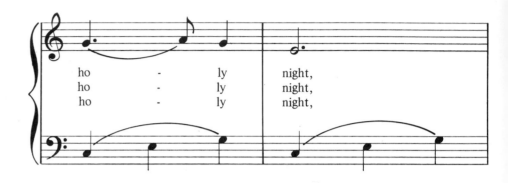

ho - ly night,
ho - ly night,
ho - ly night,

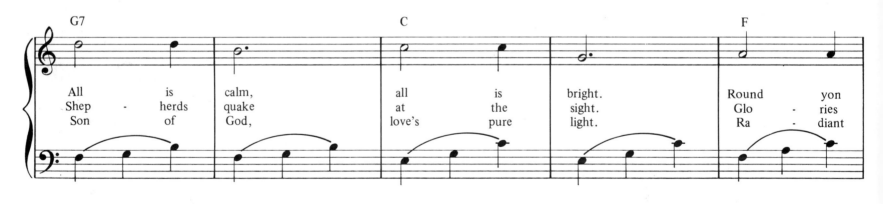

All   is   calm,   all   is   bright.   Round   yon
Shep - herds   quake   God,   at   love's   the   sight.   Glo - ries
Son   of   God,   love's   pure   light.   Ra - diant

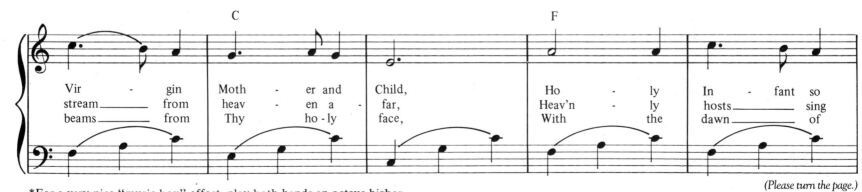

Vir - gin   Moth - er and   Child,   Ho - ly   In - fant so
stream from   heav - en a -   far,   Heav'n - ly   hosts sing
beams from   Thy   ho - ly   face,   With the   dawn of

*For a very nice "music box" effect, play both hands an octave higher.

(Please turn the page.)

Detail of an engraving from *Ethica naturalis, seu documenta moralia,*
written by Christopher Weigel (German). Published in Nuremberg, ca. 1700.

The Adoration of the Shepherds. Marcellus Coffermans, Flemish, active between 1549 and 1570. Tempera and oil on wood.

SILENT NIGHT (*continued*)

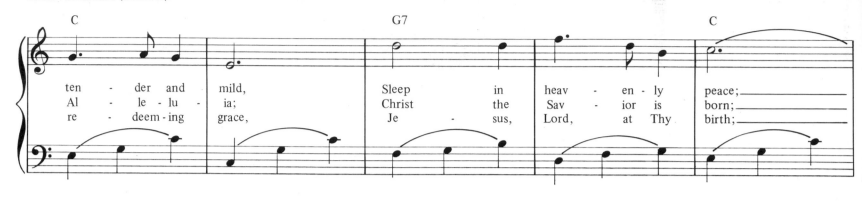

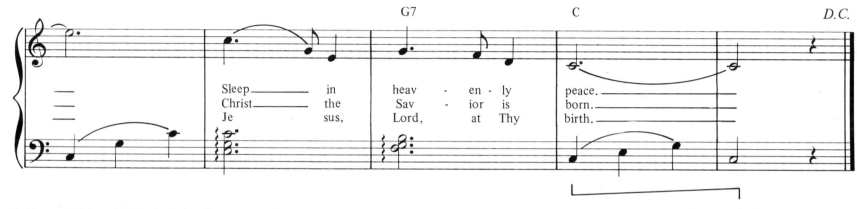

ten - der and mild,
Al - le - lu - ia;
re - deem - ing grace,

Sleep / Christ / Je in / the / sus, heav - en - ly / Sav - ior is / Lord, at Thy peace; / born; / birth;

Sleep in / Christ the / Je sus, heav - en - ly / Sav - ior is / Lord, at Thy peace. / born. / birth.

D.C.

The Nativity. Workshop of Fra Angelico, Italian (Florentine), active by 1417, d. 1455. Tempera and gold on wood.

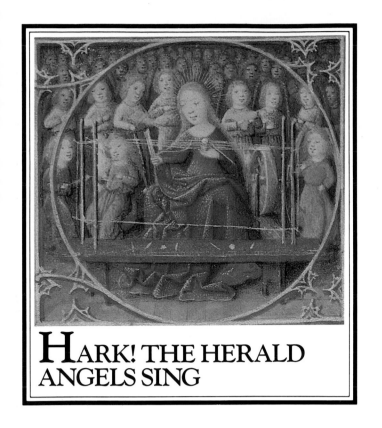

Hark! The Herald Angels Sing

Words by Charles Wesley
Music by Felix Mendelssohn

Firmly

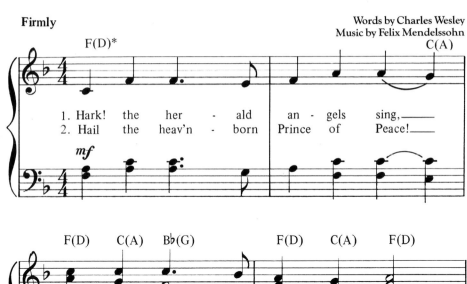

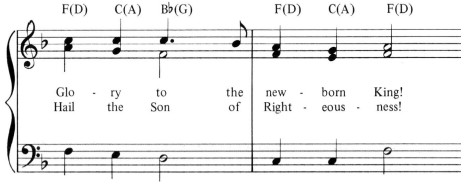

1. Hark! the her - ald an - gels sing,___
2. Hail the heav'n - born Prince of Peace!___

Glo - ry to the new - born King!
Hail the Son of Right - eous - ness!

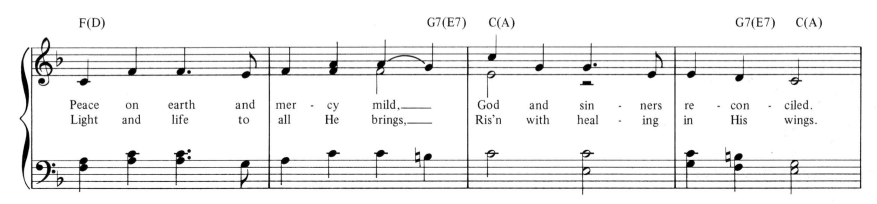

Peace on earth and mer - cy mild,___ God and sin - ners re - con - ciled.
Light and life to all He brings,___ Ris'n with heal - ing in His wings.

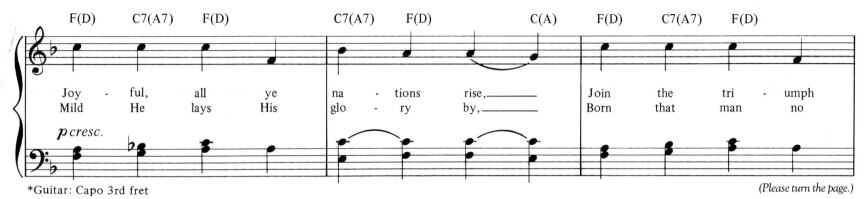

Joy - ful, all ye na - tions rise,___ Join the tri - umph
Mild He lays His glo - ry by,___ Born that man no

*Guitar: Capo 3rd fret

(Please turn the page.)

Detail of a manuscript illumination from a *Book of Hours*
made for Charles of France, Duke of Normandy. French, 1465.

13

The Annunciation: Archangel Gabriel. Manuscript illumination from a *Book of Hours* made for Charles of France, Duke of Normandy. French, 1465.

14

of the skies;
more may die.

With the an - gel - ic
Born to raise the

host pro - claim,
sons of earth;

Christ is born in Beth - le - hem!
Born to give in them sec - ond birth.

Hark! the her - ald

an - gels sing,

Glo - ry to the new - born King!

Illustration from *Nobilità di Dame . . .chiamoto Il Ballarino,* written by Fabritio Caroso da Sermoneta. Published by Presso il Muschio, Venice, 1605.

15

DECK THE HALLS

Brightly, with spirit

Welsh traditional

1. Deck the halls with boughs of hol - ly,
2. See the blaz - ing Yule be - fore us,
3. Fast a - way the old year pass - es,

Fa la la la la la la la la.

'Tis the sea - son to be jol - ly,
Strike the harp and join the cho - rus,
Hail the new, ye lads and lass - es,

Fa la la la la la la la la.

Don we now our gay ap - par - el,
Fol - low me in mer - ry mea - sure,
Sing we joy - ous all to - geth - er,

Fa la la la la la la la.

Detail of a color lithograph by Mela Koehler (Austrian, 1885–1960), published by the Wiener Werkstätte, ca. 1908–14.

16

Detail from a magazine cover by Louis Rhead (American, 1857–1926) for *Harper's Bazaar*, Christmas 1894.

HERE WE COME A-CAROLING

Joyfully, in 2 (♩ = 1 beat)   English traditional

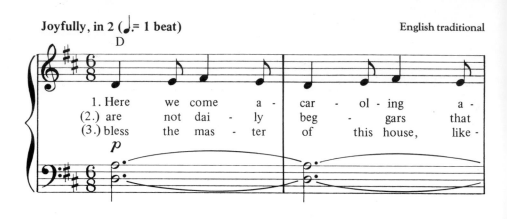

1. Here we come a-car-ol-ing a-
(2.) are not dai-ly beg-gars that
(3.) bless the mas-ter of this house, like-

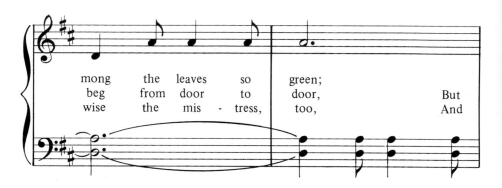

mong the leaves so green; But
beg from door to door, And
wise the mis-tress, too,

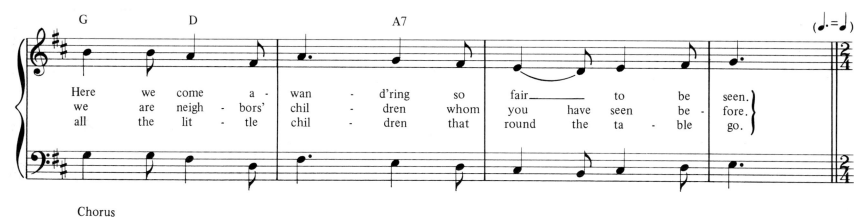

Here we come a-wan-d'ring so fair to be seen.
we are neigh-bors' chil-dren whom you have seen be-fore.
all the lit-tle chil-dren whom that round the ta-ble go.

Chorus

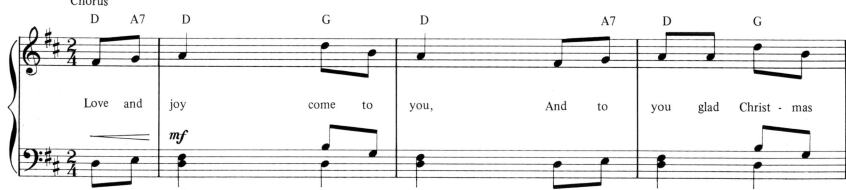

Love and joy come to you, And to you glad Christ-mas

Playing Under the Windows (detail). Cecil Aldin, British, 1870–1935.
Illustration from *Old Christmas* by Washington Irving, published by Hodder & Stoughton, London, 1908.

TOYLAND

Gently flowing

Words by Glen MacDonough
Music by Victor Herbert

*Guitar: Capo 3rd fret

(Please turn the page.)

Detail of a color lithograph by Suzi Singer-Schinnerl (Austrian, 1895–1965), published by the Wiener Werkstätte, ca. 1912.

Illustration by Wyndham
Payne (British) from *The
Mysterious Toyshop, A Fairy Tale*
by Cyril W. Beaumont.
Published in London, 1924.

Illustration by Wyndham
Payne (British) from *The
Mysterious Toyshop, A Fairy Tale*
by Cyril W. Beaumont.
Published in London, 1924.

THE FRIENDLY BEASTS

Gently   Traditional

F(D)*

1. Je - sus our broth - er,
2. "I," said the don - key,
3. "I," said the cow,

p - mp

C7(A7)   F(D)

kind and good, was
shag - gy and brown, "I
white and red, "I

Bb(G)   F(D)

hum - bly born in a sta - ble rude, And the
car - ried His moth - er up hill and down; I
gave Him my man - ger for a bed; I

C7(A7)   F(D)   C7(A7)   F(D)

friend - ly beasts a - round Him stood,
car - ried her safe - ly to Beth - le - hem town."
gave Him my hay to pil - low His head."

*Guitar: Capo 3rd fret

The Creation of the Animals. Detail of a stained-glass panel. Swiss, 1694.

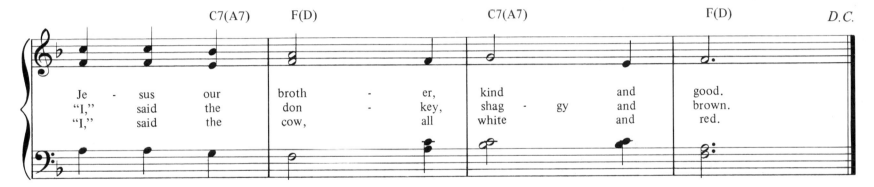

	C7(A7)	F(D)		C7(A7)		F(D)	*D.C.*

Je - sus our broth - er, kind and good.
"I," said the don - key, shag - gy and brown.
"I," said the cow, all white and red.

Additional verses:

4.
"I," said the sheep with curly horn,
"I gave Him my wool for His blanket warm;
He wore my coat on Christmas morn.
I," said the sheep with curly horn.

5.
"I," said the dove from the rafters high,
"Cooed Him to sleep that He should not cry;
We cooed Him to sleep, my mate and I.
I," said the dove from the rafters high.

6.
"I," said the camel, yellow and black,
"Over the desert, upon my back,
I brought Him a gift in the Wise Men's pack.
I," said the camel, yellow and black.

7.
Thus every beast by some good spell,
In the stable dark was glad to tell
Of the gift he gave Emmanuel,
The gift he gave Emmanuel.

The Nativity (detail). Antoniazzo Romano (Antonio di Benedetto Aquilio), Italian (Roman), active by 1452, d. by 1512. Tempera on wood.

JINGLE BELLS

With spirit   Words and music by James Pierpont

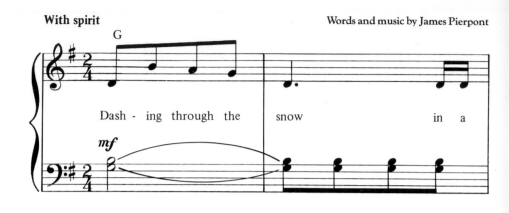

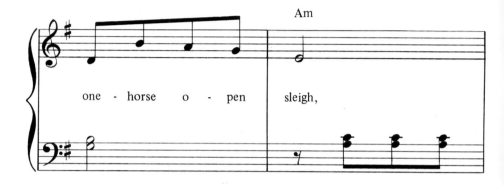

Detail of a color lithograph by Valerie Petter (Austrian, 1881–1963), published by the Wiener Werkstätte, ca. 1908.

fun it is to ride and sing a sleigh-ing song to-night. Oh!

Chorus

Jin - gle bells! Jin - gle bells! Jin - gle all the way!

(Please turn the page.)

The Sleigh Race. Detail of a hand-colored lithograph published by Currier & Ives, New York, 1859.

Oh, what fun it is to ride in a one - horse o - pen sleigh, hey!

Jin - gle bells! Jin - gle bells! Jin - gle all the way!

Oh, what fun it is to ride in a one - horse o - pen sleigh! Hey!

Adaptation of drawings in ink and watercolor made for Brewster and Co., New York. American, late 19th century.

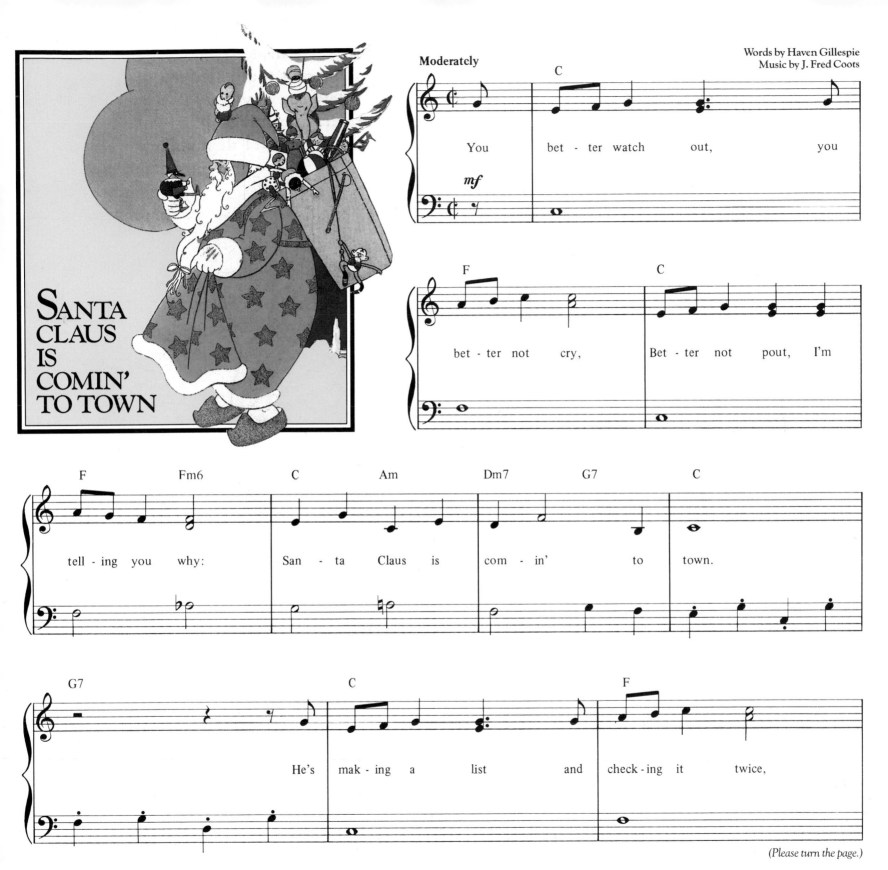

SANTA CLAUS IS COMIN' TO TOWN

Words by Haven Gillespie
Music by J. Fred Coots

Moderately

mf

You bet-ter watch out, you bet-ter not cry, Bet-ter not pout, I'm tell-ing you why: San-ta Claus is com-in' to town.

He's mak-ing a list and check-ing it twice,

(Please turn the page.)

Santa (detail). Jean Ray, French. Hand-colored illustration from "Conte de Noël," in *La Guirlande: Album d'Art et de Littérature,* published in Paris, 1920.

Gon-na find out who's naugh-ty and nice: San-ta Claus is

com-in' to town. He sees you when you're

Woodcut illustrations by Edgard Tijtgat, Belgian, 1879–1957.
From *Le Lendemain de la Saint-Nicolas*,
published by Remy Havermans, Brussels, 1913.

O COME, ALL YE FAITHFUL

Moderately

Words by Frederick Oakeley (English) and John Frances Wade (Latin)
Music by John Reading

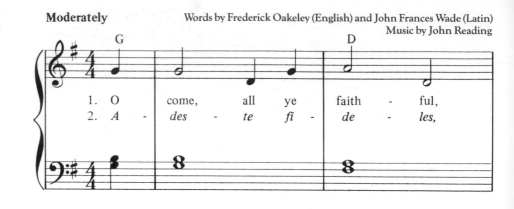

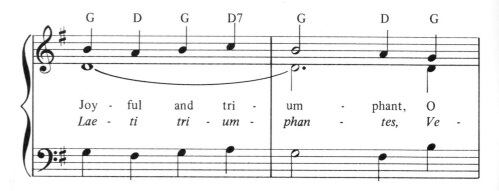

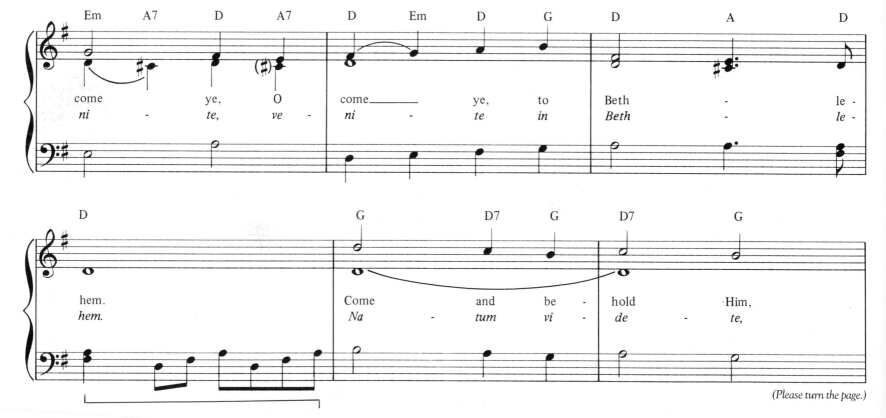

1. O come, all ye faith - ful,
2. *A - des - te fi - de - les,*

Joy - ful and tri - um - phant, O
Lae - ti tri - um - phan - tes, Ve -

come ye, O come_____ ye, to Beth - le -
ni - te, ve - ni - te in Beth - le -

hem.
hem.

Come and be - hold Him,
Na - tum vi - de - te,

(Please turn the page.)

Detail of a color lithograph by Josef von Divéky (Austrian, 1887–1951), published by the Wiener Werkstätte, 1908.

Illustration by Jeanne Kerremans (Belgian, active 1930s) from *Le Manteau de Roi et autres Contes de Noël* by Camille Melloy. Published by Desclée, de Brouwer, Brussels, 1939.

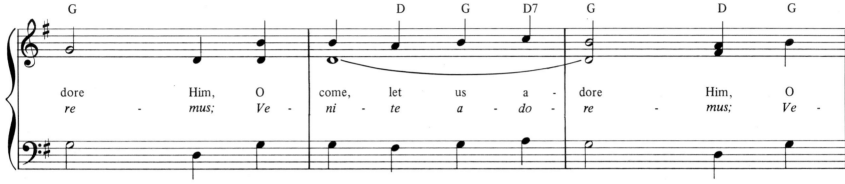

born the King of an - gels. O come, let us a -	
Re - *gem* *an* - *ge* - *lo* - *rum.* *Ve* - *ni* - *te* *a* - *do*	

dore   Him,   O   come,   let   us   a -   dore   Him,   O
re - *mus;*   *Ve* - *ni* - *te*   *a* - *do* - *re* - *mus;*   *Ve* -

come,   let   us   a -   dore   Him,_____   Christ_____   the   Lord.
ni - *te*   *a* - *do* - *re* - *mus,_____*   *Do* - *mi* - *num.*

Additional verses:

3. Sing, choirs of angels,
   Sing in exultation;
   Sing all ye citizens of heav'n above:
   Glory to God in the highest.
   O come, let us adore Him,
   O come, let us adore Him,
   O come, let us adore Him, Christ, the Lord.

4. Yea, Lord, we greet Thee,
   Born this happy morning;
   Jesus, to Thee be glory giv'n;
   Word of the Father, now in flesh appearing.
   O come, let us adore Him,
   O come, let us adore Him,
   O come, let us adore Him, Christ, the Lord.

Detail from a woodcut, *Rest on the Flight into Egypt,* by Lucas Cranach the Elder, German, 1472–1553.

O HOLY NIGHT

Words by John Sullivan Dwight
Music by Adolphe Adam

Slowly, in 2 (♩ = 1 beat)

O ho - ly night,_____ the stars are bright - ly shin - ing; It is the night of the dear Sav - ior's birth._____ Long lay the

Annunciation to the Shepherds (detail). Henri Rivière, French, 1864–1951. Color lithograph from a broadside for *La Marche à l'Etoile* by Georges Fragerolle.

(Please turn the page.)

Nativity with the Annunciation to the Shepherds. Follower of Jan Joest of Calcar, Flemish, active by 1505, d. 1519. Oil on wood.

O HOLY NIGHT (continued)

world _____ in sin and er - ror pin - ing, Till He ap- peared and the soul felt its worth. _____ A thrill of hope, the wea - ry soul re - joic - es, For yon - der breaks a new and glo - rious morn.

flowing *p*

(Please turn the page.)

O HOLY NIGHT (*continued*)

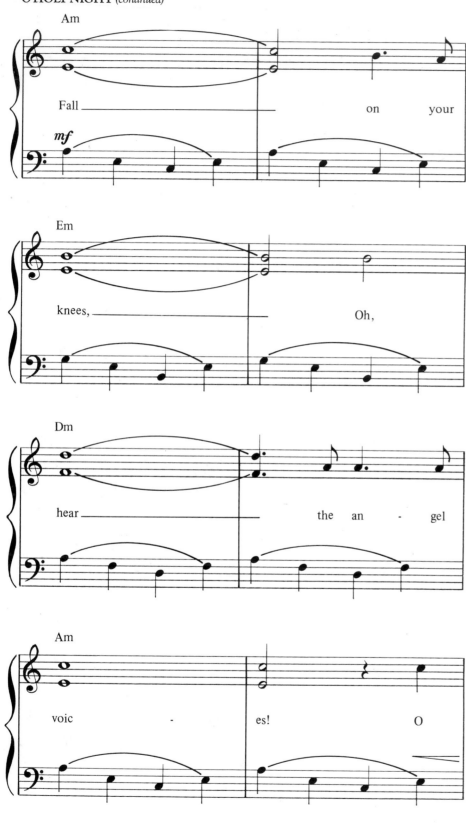

Virgin and Child. Rhenish or Bohemian, first quarter of the 15th century. Wood, polychromed and gilt.

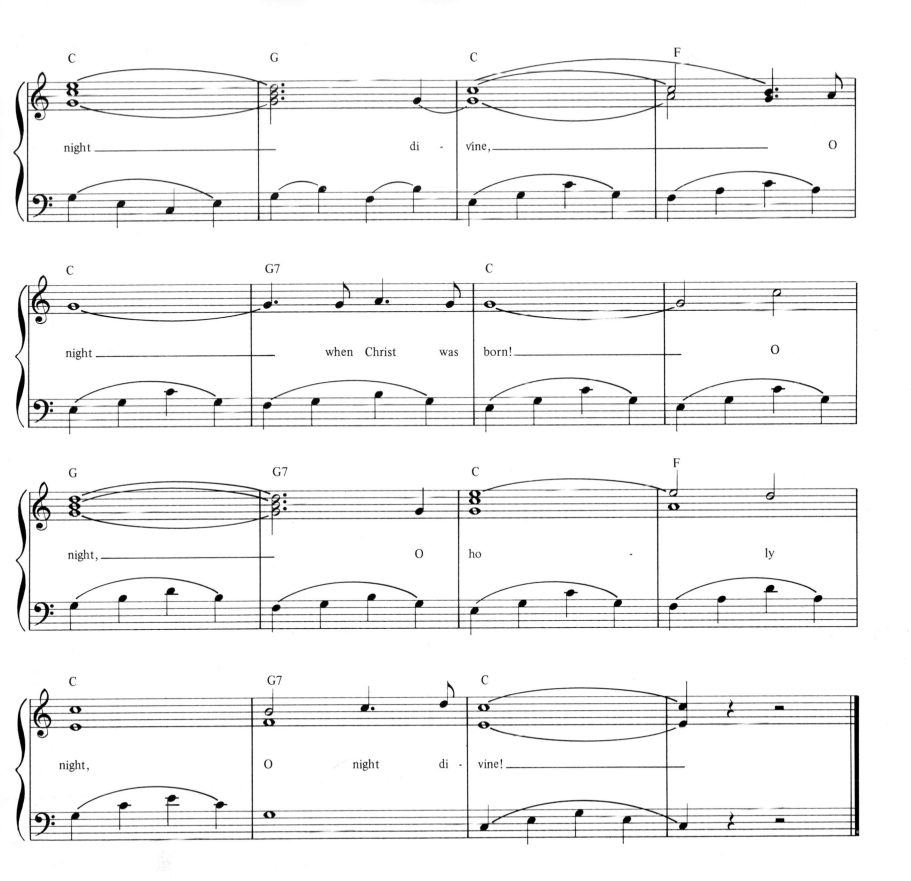

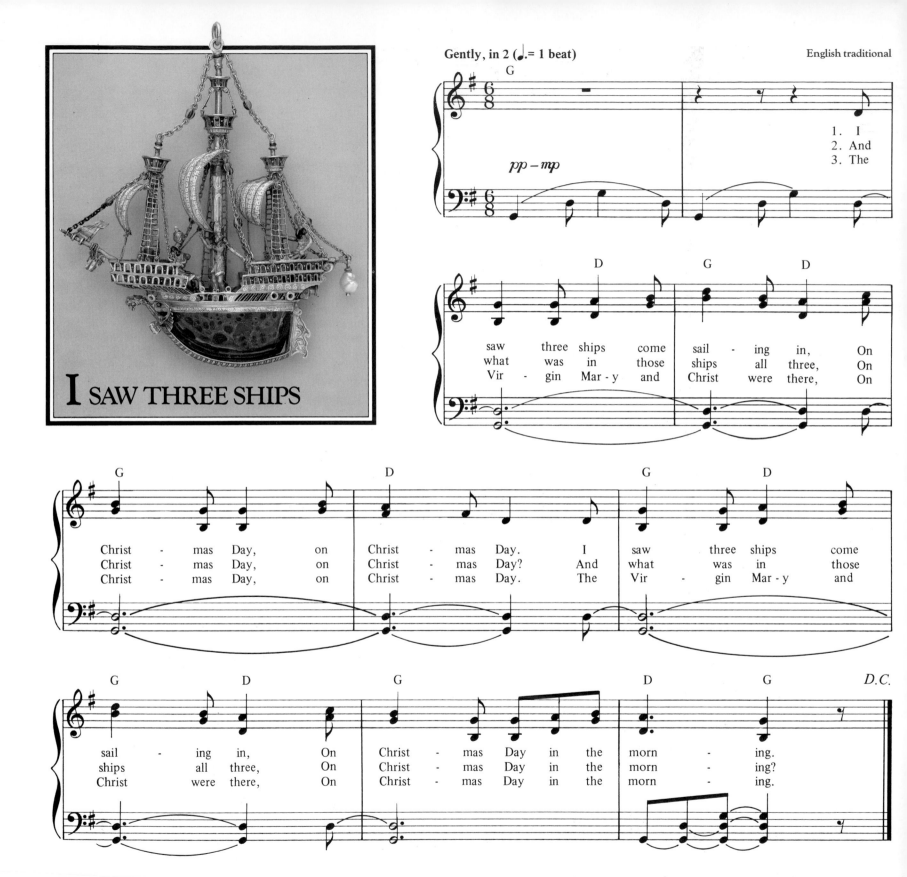

I SAW THREE SHIPS

Gently, in 2 (♩.= 1 beat)   English traditional

pp – mp

1. I
2. And
3. The

saw   three ships come | sail - ing in, On
what was   in   those | ships all three, On
Vir - gin Mar - y and | Christ all were there, On

Christ - mas Day, on | Christ - mas Day. I | saw three ships come
Christ - mas Day, on | Christ - mas Day? And | what was in those
Christ - mas Day, on | Christ - mas Day. The | Vir - gin Mar - y and

sail - ing in, On | Christ - mas Day in the | morn - ing.
ships all three, On | Christ - mas Day in the | morn - ing?
Christ were there, On | Christ - mas Day in the | morn - ing.

D.C.

Ship pendant. Probably southern European, second half of the 16th century. Gold, partially enameled, and painted rock crystal, with a pearl.

Detail of an illustration by
Francis D. Bedford (British,
1864–1934) for "I Saw Three
Ships," from *A Book of
Nursery Rhymes*, published
by Doubleday & McClure
Co., New York, 1897.

O CHRISTMAS TREE

German traditional

Firmly

f

mf

| N.C. | F(D)* | C7(A7) | F(D) | | Gm7(Em7) | C7(A7) | F(D) N.C. |

1. O Christ - mas tree, O Christ - mas tree, you stand in ver - dant beau - ty. O
2. O Christ - mas tree, O Christ - mas tree, you fill all hearts with gai - ety. O

| F(D) | C7(A7) | F(D) | | Gm7(Em7) | C7(A7) | F(D) |

Christ - mas tree, O Christ - mas tree, you stand in ver - dant beau - ty. Your
Christ - mas tree, O Christ - mas tree, you fill all hearts with gai - ety. On

p

*Guitar: Capo 3rd fret

(*Please turn the page.*)

Detail of a color lithograph by Josef von Divéky (Austrian, 1887–1951), published by the Wiener Werkstätte, ca. 1908.

Christmas tree at The Metropolitan Museum of Art. Decorated with dressed figures of polychromed terracotta and wood. Italian (Neapolitan), late 18th–early 19th century.

O CHRISTMAS TREE (*continued*)

boughs are green in summer's glow, And
Christ - mas Day in you stand so tall, Af -

do not fade in winter's snow. O
ford - ing joy to one and all. O

Christ - mas tree, O Christ - mas tree, You
Christ - mas tree, O Christ - mas tree, You

stand in ver - dant beau - ty.
fill all hearts with gai - ety.

Detail of the Christmas tree at The Metropolitan Museum of Art.

WE THREE KINGS OF ORIENT ARE

Moderately flowing

Words and music by John Henry Hopkins

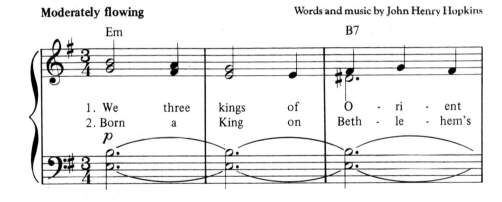

Em — B7

1. We three kings of O - ri - ent
2. Born a King on Beth - le - hem's

p

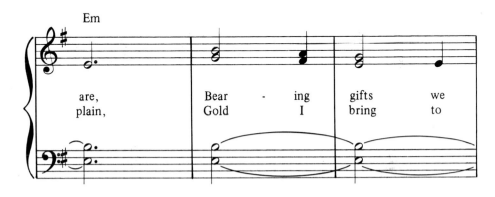

Em

are, Bear - ing gifts we
plain, Gold I bring we to

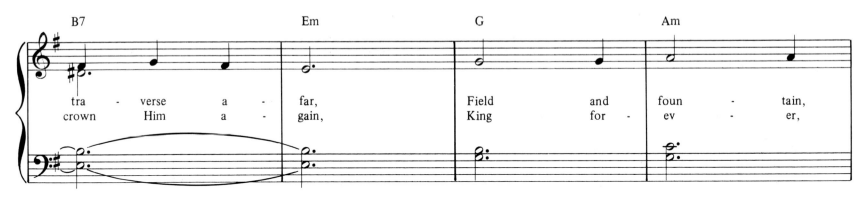

B7 — Em — G — Am

tra - verse a - far, Field and foun - tain,
crown Him a - gain, King for - ev - er,

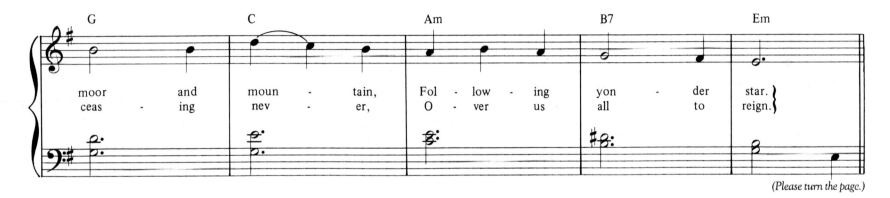

G — C — Am — B7 — Em

moor and moun - tain, Fol - low - ing yon - der star.
ceas - ing nev - er, O - ver us all to reign.

(Please turn the page.)

The Three Kings. Detail from a tile. Dutch, 18th century. Tin-enameled earthenware.

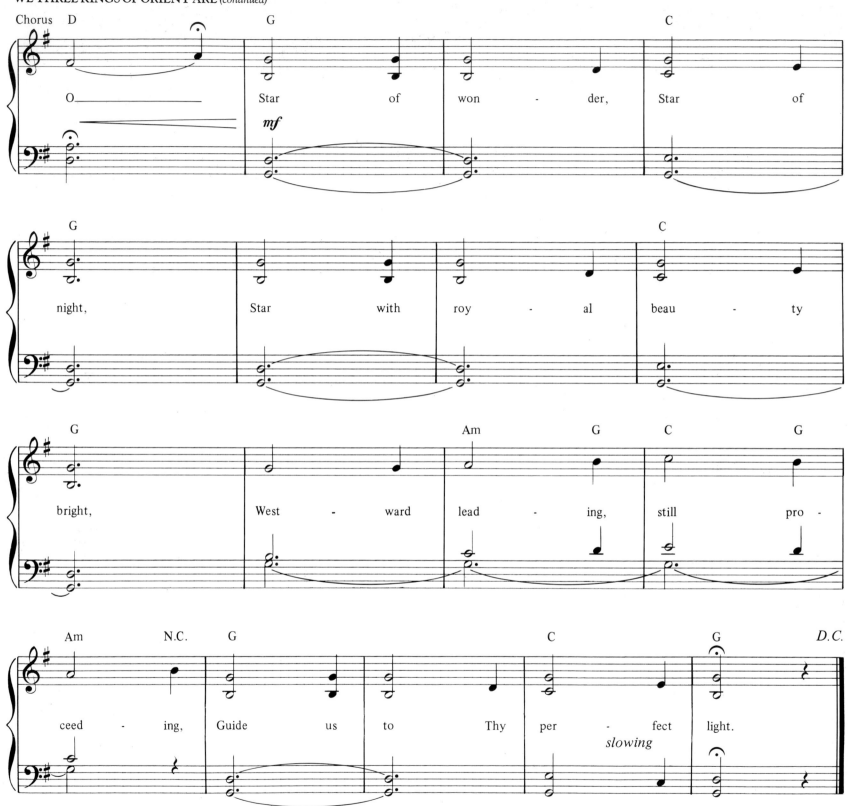

The Journey of the Magi. Sassetta (Stefano di Giovanni), Italian (Sienese), active by 1423, d. 1450. Tempera and gold on wood.

Additional verses:

3. Frankincense to offer have I,
   Incense owns a Deity nigh.
   Pray'r and praising, all men raising,
   Worship Him, God most high.

   (*Chorus*)

4. Myrrh is mine, its bitter perfume
   Breathes a life of gathering gloom;
   Sorrowing, sighing, bleeding, dying,
   Sealed in the stone-cold tomb.

   (*Chorus*)

5. Glorious now behold him arise,
   King and God and sacrifice.
   Alleluia, Alleluia,
   Earth to heav'ns replies.

   (*Chorus*)

Words by Edmund Hamilton Sears   Music by Richard Storrs Willis

It Came Upon the Midnight Clear

Gently, in 2 (♩.= 1 beat)

1. It came upon the mid-night clear, that
2. Still through the clo-ven skies they come, with

glo-ri-ous song of old, From
peace-ful wings un-furl'd; And

an-gels bend-ing near the earth to touch their harps of
still their heav'n-ly mu-sic floats o'er all the wea-ry

gold. Peace on the earth, good will to men from
world: A-bove its sad and low-ly plains they

*Guitar: Capo 3rd fret

Dante and Beatrice with the Blessed Souls (detail). Woodcut from *Comedia dell'Inferno, del Purgatorio, e del Paradiso*, by Dante Alighieri. Published by Giovambattista Marchiò Sessa et Fratelli, Venice, 1578.

48

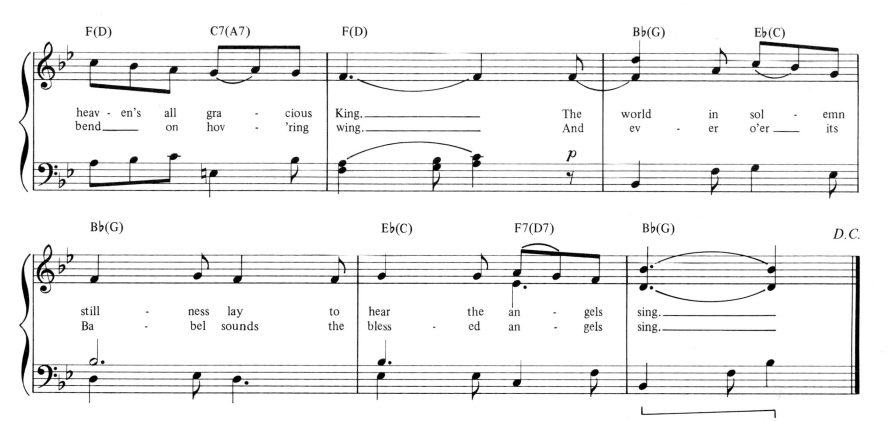

The Way Home (detail). Ludwig Michaelek, Austrian, 1859–1942. Color etching and aquatint, 1901.

The Nativity (detail). Woodcut from *Meditations on the Life of Christ*. Italian (Venetian), 1576.

(Please turn the page.)

The Adoration of the Magi. Hieronymus Bosch, Flemish, active by 1480, d. 1516. Tempera and oil on wood.

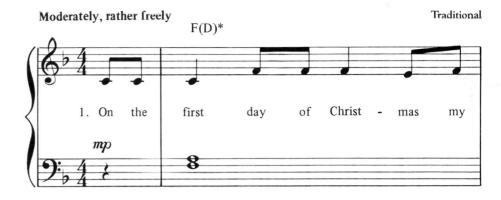

Moderately, rather freely   Traditional

THE TWELVE DAYS OF CHRISTMAS

1. On the first day of Christ-mas my true love sent to me a par-tridge in a pear tree.

2. On the sec-ond day of Christ-mas my true love sent to me two tur-tle-doves and a par-tridge in a pear

*Guitar: Capo 3rd fret

(Please turn the page.)

Detail of an illustration from a tournament manuscript. German (Nuremberg), late 16th century. Ink and watercolor with gold.

tree._____ 3. On the third day of Christ - mas my true love sent to me

three French_ hens, two tur - tle - doves, and a par - tridge_ in a pear

tree._____ 4. On the fourth day of Christ - mas my true love sent to me

four call - ing birds, three French_ hens, two tur - tle - doves, and a

(Please turn the page.)

Embroidered textile. English, first half of the 17th century. Silk on canvas.

par - tridge__ in a pear tree._____ 5. On the fifth day of Christ - mas my

Broadly

true love sent to me five gold - en rings, four__ call - ing birds,

Briskly, as before

three French hens, two__ tur - tle - doves, and a par - tridge__ in a pear tree._____ 6. On the

Adaptation of a color lithograph by Rudolf Kalvack (Austrian, 1883–1932), published by the Wiener Werkstätte, ca. 1908.

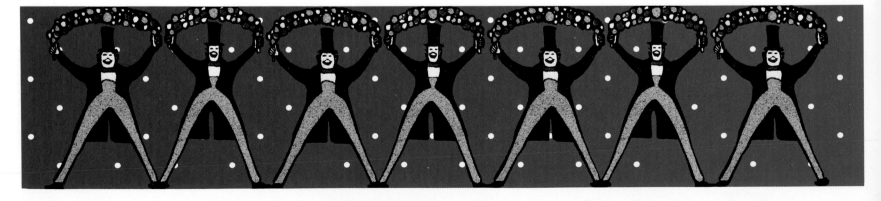

THE FIRST NOEL

Moderately

G   C   G

mf

1. The first No - el the
2. They look - ed up and
3. And by the light of

F   C

an - gel did say, Was to
saw a star star shin - ing
that same star Three

F   C F G7 C   G7 C   G

cer - tain poor shep - herds in fields as they lay; In
in the east be - yond them far; And
wise men came from coun - try far; To

C   G   F   C

fields where they lay keep - ing their sheep On a
to the earth it gave great light And
seek for a king was their in - tent, And to

(Please turn the page.)

Detail of a color lithograph by Oscar Kokoschka (Austrian, 1886–1980),
published by the Wiener Werkstätte, 1906–08.

Annunciation to the Shepherds. Detail from a wool tapestry.
German (Upper Rhine), late 15th century.

Chorus

cold   win - ter's   night _____   that   was _____   so   deep.

so   it   con -   tin - ued   that   both   day _____   and   night.

fol - low   the   star _____   wher - ev - er   it   went.

No -

el, _____   No - el,   No - el,   No - el,

Born   is   the   King _____   of   Is - ra - el.

D.C.

Two angels. Detail from an undyed linen and wool tapestry curtain. Egyptian (Coptic), 6th century.

GOD REST YE MERRY, GENTLEMEN

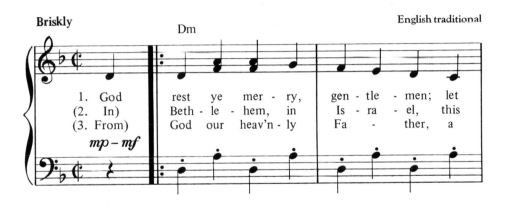

Briskly

English traditional

Dm

1. God rest ye mer - ry, gen - tle - men; let
(2. In) Beth - le - hem, in Is - ra - el, this
(3. From) God our heav'n - ly Fa - ther, a

mp – mf

noth - ing you dis - may. Re -
bless - ed Babe was born, And
bless - ed an - gel came; And

mem - ber, Christ our Sav - ior was born on Christ - mas Day To
laid with - in a man - ger up - on this bless - ed morn; The
un - to cer - tain shep - herds brought ti - dings of the same; How

Gm · C · F · A7 · Dm · Dm7 · G · **Chorus** Gm

save us all from Sa - tan's pow'r when we were gone a - stray. } O____
which His Moth - er Mar - y did noth - ing take in scorn.
that in Beth - le - hem was born the Son of God by name.

(Please turn the page.)

Woodcut by Allen Lewis, American, 1873–1957.

The Nativity. Center panel from a triptych
by Gerard David, Flemish, active by 1484, d. 1523.
Tempera and oil on canvas, transferred from wood.

Detail of an illuminated manuscript page from the
Belles Heures of Jean, Duke of Berry. Jean, Pol, and Herman de Limbourg,
French (Paris), active ca. 1400–1416. Tempera and gold on vellum.

GOOD KING WENCESLAS

Words by John Mason Neale
Music traditional

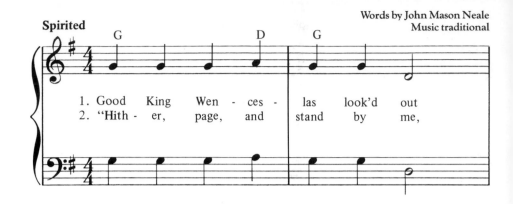

Spirited

1. Good King Wen - ces - las look'd out
2. "Hith - er, page, and stand by me,

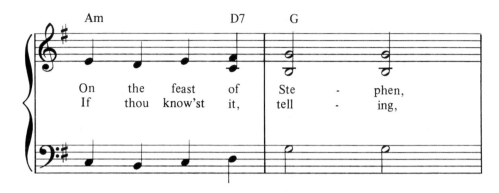

On the feast of Ste - phen,
If thou know'st it, tell - ing,

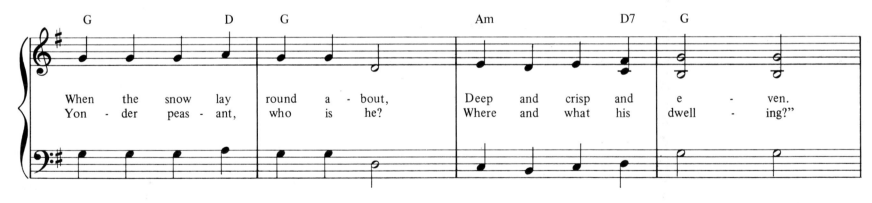

When the snow lay round a - bout, Deep and crisp and e - ven.
Yon - der peas - ant, who is he? Where and what his dwell - ing?"

Bright - ly shone the moon that night, Though the frost was cru - el,
"Sire, he lives a good league hence, Un - der - neath the moun - tain;

Details of two color lithographs by Carl Krenek (Austrian, 1880–1948), published by the Wiener Werkstätte, ca. 1912.

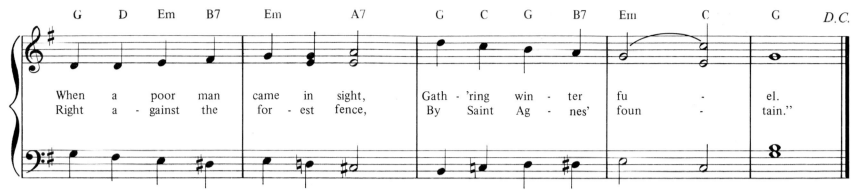

	G	D	Em	B7	Em	A7	G	C	G	B7	Em	C	G	*D.C.*

When a poor man came in sight, Gath - 'ring win - ter fu - el.
Right a - gainst the for - est fence, By Saint Ag - nes' foun - tain."

Additional verses:

3. "Bring me flesh and bring me wine,
    Bring me pine logs hither.
    Thou and I will see him dine,
    When we bear him thither."
    Page and monarch forth they went,
    Forth they went together,
    Through the rude wind's wild lament,
    And the bitter weather.

4. "Sire, the night is darker now,
    And the wind blows stronger.
    Fails my heart, I know not how,
    I can go no longer."
    "Mark my footsteps, my good page,
    Tread thou in them boldly.
    Thou shalt find the winter's rage
    Freeze thy blood less coldly."

5. In his master's steps he trod,
    When the snow lay dinted.
    Heat was in the very sod
    Which the Saint had printed.
    Therefore, Christian men, be sure,
    Wealth or rank possessing,
    Ye who now will bless the poor,
    Shall yourselves find blessing.

Joyously

French traditional

F				C7 F		C F

1. An - gels we have heard on high, Sweet - ly sing - ing
2. Shep - herds, why this ju - bi - lee? Why your joy - ous
3. Come to Beth - le - hem and see Him whose birth the

mf

C7 F		C7 F

o'er the plains, And the moun - tains in re - ply,
strains pro - long? What the glad - some ti - dings be,
an - gels sing. Come a - dore on bend - ed knee

(Please turn the page.)

Detail of a color lithograph by Franz Karl Delavilla
(Austrian, 1884–1967), published by the Wiener Werkstätte, 1908.

Annunciation to the Shepherds. Illuminated manuscript page from the *Belles Heures* of Jean, Duke of Berry.
Jean, Pol, and Herman de Limbourg, French (Paris), active ca. 1400–1416. Tempera and gold on vellum.

eus in ad   Domine ad adiu
iutorium   uandum me festina.
meum in   Gloria pri et filio
tende.   et spiritui sancto.

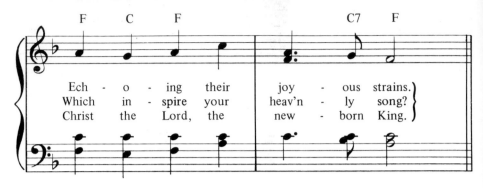

Ech - o - ing their joy - ous strains.
Which in - spire your heav'n - ly song?
Christ the Lord, the new - born King.

Chorus

Glo -

mf

- ri - a

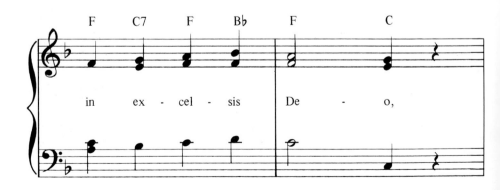

in ex - cel - sis De - o,

Detail of a border design by Aubrey Beardsley (British, 1872–1898) for *Le Morte d'Arthur* by Sir Thomas Malory, 1893–94. Drawing in ink on paper.

JOY TO THE WORLD!

Majestically

Words by Isaac Watts   Music by Lowell Mason

1. Joy to the world! the Lord is come: Let earth re- ceive her King. Let ev- 'ry heart pre- pare Him room, And
2. Joy to the world! the Sav- ior reigns: Let men their songs em- ploy, While ev- fields and floods, rocks, hills, plains, Re-
3. He rules the world with truth and grace, And makes the na- tions prove His glo- ries, And of right- eous- ness, And

f

p cresc.

(Please turn the page.)

Christmas Carolers (detail). Ludwig Richter, German, 1803–1884. Wood engraving.

Virgin and Child with Saint John the Baptist and Angels. François Boucher, French, 1703–1770. Oil on canvas, 1765.

70

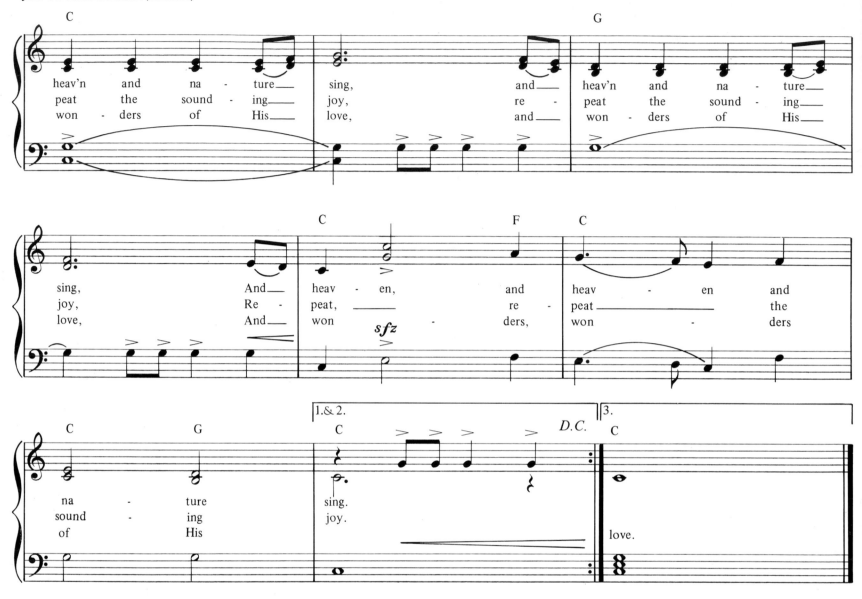

heav'n and na - ture sing, and heav'n and na - ture
peat the sound - ing joy, re - peat the sound - ing
won - ders of His love, and won - ders of His

sing, And heav - en, and heav - en and
joy, Re - peat, and re - peat the
love, And won - ders, won - ders

na - ture sing.
sound - ing joy.
of His love.

Detail from a woodcut, *Rest on the Flight into Egypt,* by Lucas Cranach the Elder, German, 1472–1553.

WE WISH YOU A MERRY CHRISTMAS

Joyfully

English traditional

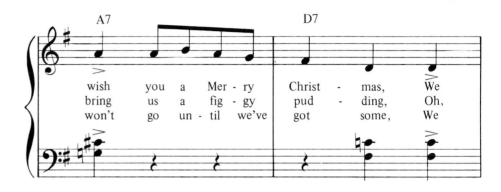

1. We wish you a Mer-ry Christ-mas, We
2. Oh, bring us a fig-gy pud-ding, Oh,
3. We won't go un-til we've got some, We

wish you a Mer-ry Christ-mas, We
bring us a fig-gy pud-ding, Oh,
won't go un-til we've got some, We

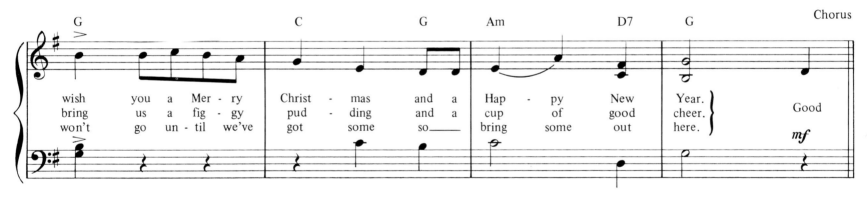

wish you a Mer-ry Christ-mas and a Hap-py New Year. } Good
bring us a fig-gy pud-ding and a cup of good cheer.
won't go un-til we've got some so___ bring some out here.

Chorus

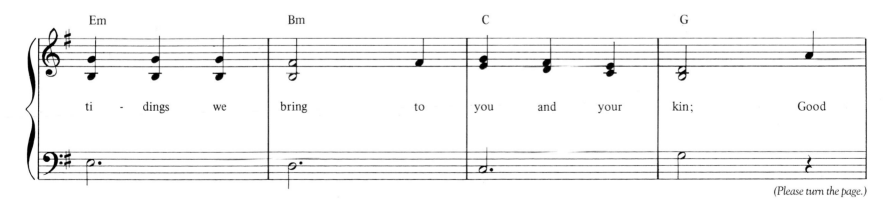

ti-dings we bring to you and your kin; Good

(Please turn the page.)

Detail of an illustration by Randolph Caldecott (British, 1846–1886) from *Gleanings from the "Graphic,"* London, 1889.

WE WISH YOU A MERRY CHRISTMAS (continued)

ti - dings for Christ - mas and a Hap - py New Year.

Last time only

We wish you a Mer - ry Christ - mas, We wish you a Mer - ry Christ - mas, We

wish you a Mer - ry Christ - mas and a Hap - py New Year.

slower

Christmas-Time (The Blodgett Family). Eastman Johnson, American, 1824–1906. Oil on canvas, 1864.

Illustrations by Arthur Rackham (British, 1867–1939) for *Cinderella,* retold by C. S. Evans. Published by William Heinemann, London, and J. B. Lippincott Co., Philadelphia, 1919.

Auld Lang Syne

Words by Robert Burns
Music traditional

Moderately

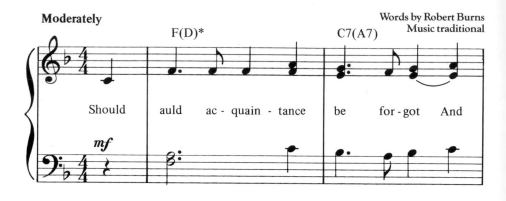

Should auld ac-quain-tance be for-got And

nev-er brought to mind? Should

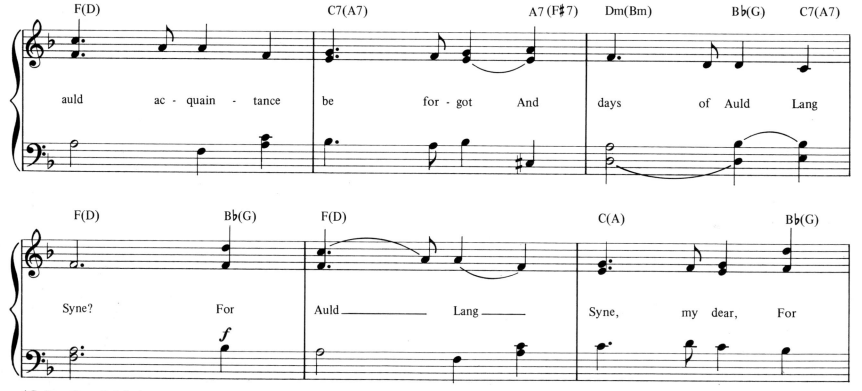

auld ac-quain-tance be for-got And days of Auld Lang

Syne? For Auld——— Lang——— Syne, my dear, For

*Guitar: Capo 3rd fret

Detail of a color lithograph published by the Wiener Werkstätte, ca. 1914.

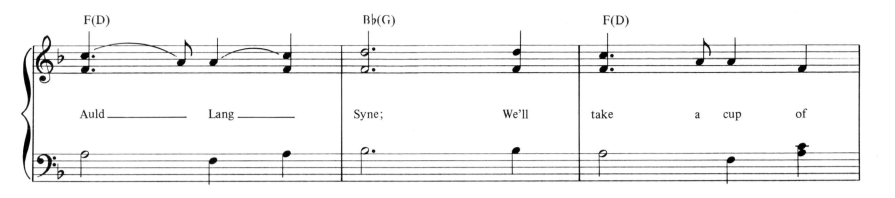

Auld _____ Lang _____ Syne; We'll take a cup of

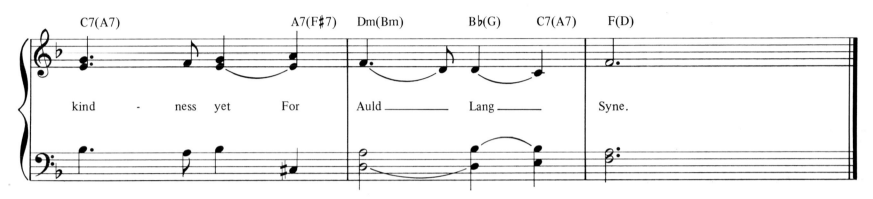

kind - ness yet For Auld _____ Lang _____ Syne.

Adaptation from *The Marriage Feast at Cana.* Anders Pålsson, Swedish, 1781–1849. Painted linen wall hanging, 1818.

CREDITS

INDEX OF FIRST LINES

GUITAR CHORD DIAGRAMS

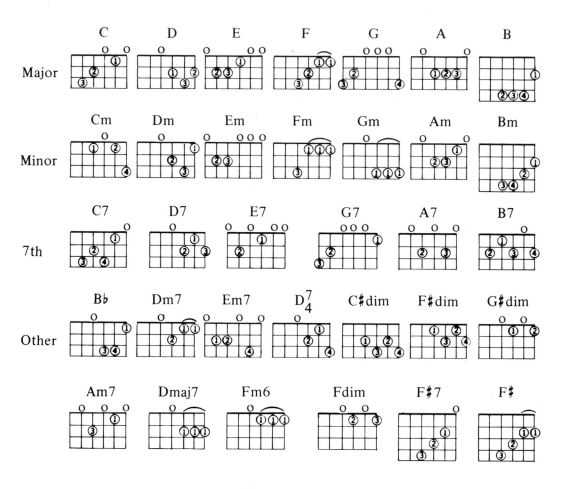